MOTOR VEHICLE LOGBOOK

VEHICLE:

____

Logbook number _______________

Entries from _______________

Through _______________

www.parhelionaerospace.com
Author: Michael L. Rampey
ISBN: 978-2-8399-3356-8

Holder of this Logbook / Vehicle Responsible Person

Holder's Identity (The Holder is the person who will sign the logbook pages, certifying their accuracy).	
Holder's Name:	Owner of Vehicle Logged in This Book:
Holder's Address / Contact Information:	Change of Holder's Address / Contact Information:
Change of Holder's Address / Contact Information:	Change of Holder's Address / Contact Information:

Contents

Part 1: Vehicle and Equipment Data

Vehicle Identification Data

Permanent Identity	Changeable Identity
Make:	Private or Commercial Use:
Model:	Place of Registration:
Year of Manufacture:	Date of Registration:
Use Type: (e.g. Passenger, Cargo, Utility):	Registration / License Plate Number:
Body Style (e.g. SUV, Convertible):	Exterior / Interior Finish:
Power Source / Fuel: (e.g. Electricity, Gasoline):	Modifications (e.g. Lift Kit, Engine Mod.):
Empty Weight:	
Vehicle Identification Number:	

Vehicle Identification Data; extra

Changeable Identity	Changeable Identity
Private or Commercial Use:	Private or Commercial Use:
Place of Registration:	Place of Registration:
Date of Registration:	Date of Registration:
Registration / License Plate Number:	Registration / License Plate Number:
Exterior / Interior Finish:	Exterior / Interior Finish:
Modifications (e.g. Lift Kit, Engine Mod.):	Modifications (e.g. Lift Kit, Engine Mod.):

Equipment

Item Description (e.g. First aid Kit, Fire Extinguisher, Jerry Can)	Date Acquired
1	
2	
3	
4	
5	
6	
7	
8	
9	
10	

Equipment, continued

Item Description (e.g. First aid Kit, Fire Extinguisher, Jerry Can)	Date Acquired
11	
12	
13	
14	
15	
16	
17	
18	
19	
20	

INSURANCE

Initial Policy	Change of Policy
Insurer:	Insurer:
Policy Number:	Policy Number:
Type of Coverage:	Type of Coverage:
Coverage Period:	Coverage Period:
Agent's Name:	Agent's Name:
Agent / Insurer Contact Info:	Agent / Insurer Contact Info:

Insurance, continued

Change of Policy	Change of Policy
Insurer:	Insurer:
Policy Number:	Policy Number:
Type of Coverage:	Type of Coverage:
Coverage Period:	Coverage Period:
Agent's Name:	Agent's Name:
Agent / Insurer Contact Info:	Agent / Insurer Contact Info:

Vehicle Owner Data

Owner (for commercial ownership, enter business name)	Owner Update (for commercial ownership, enter business name)
Name:	Owner Contact Info:
Date Vehicle Acquired:	
Place of Purchase:	
Seller's Name:	
Odometer at Purchase:	
Owner Contact Info.:	Owner Contact Info:

Subsequent Owners Data

Subsequent Owner (for commercial ownership, enter business name)	Subs. Owner Update (for commercial ownership, enter business name)
Name:	Owner Contact Info:
Date Vehicle Acquired:	
Place of Purchase:	
Seller's Name:	
Odometer at Purchase:	
Owner Contact Info.:	Owner Contact Info:

Basic Reference Data

Item	Reference Details (e.g. Type, Brand, Amount, Duration of Use, Change Interval - use blank sections as required)
Battery	
Tires / Tyres	
Fuel	
Engine Oil	
Engine Coolant	
Transmission Fluid	

Part 2: Trips Log

How to log information in the Trips Log

Specifically, the '**Vehicle Use Log**' pages (example provided on page 20)

Trip No. Enter the number of the Trip (e.g. 1, 2, 3, or T1, T2, T3, etc, in accordance with individual or company practices). This number is the reference used when writing corresponding remarks and data in the associated **Trips Details** page.

Date Enter the month and day of the Trip. Use MM/DD or DD/MM format as desired. The year is recorded separately at the top of the page.

Driver's Name / Signature Print or sign the name of the vehicle driver for the given Trip.

Trip From / To: Enter the departure and arrival locations of the given Trip.

Odometer Departure / Arrival: Enter the odometer readings at the places of departure and arrival for the given Trip.

Distance Business / Private: Enter the distances driven for business or private purposes.
Total: Enter the total distance driven for each entry. If a given trip was partially business and partially private, sum those values and enter the sum in the space provided.

Vehicle Use Log notes continue on the next page →

Specifically, the '**Vehicle Use Log**' pages (example provided on page 20)

Totals this page: Enter the totals of each of the Distance columns in the spaces provided.

Totals brought forward: Copy here the '**Totals to Date'** figure from the previous **Vehicle Use Log** page.

Totals to Date: Sum the 'Totals this page' and the 'Totals brought forward' figures on the given page. These are your current total vehicle use values.

% of **Total** distance driven that was for business: Use the **Totals to Date** figures to calculate the percentage of travel distance that was for business purposes.

% of **Total** distance driven that was private: Use the **Totals to Date** figures to calculate the percentage of travel distance that was for private, or non-business, purposes.

Business costs total: Use the appropriate Costs values from the **Trips Details** page to calculate the amount of operating costs that should be designated as Business expenses, in accordance with your business practices. For example, you may chose to apply the business distance percentage to the **Total Cost** value as representing an approximation of business expense. Alternatively, you may choose to sum those expenses that occurred during the trips designated as business travel and enter that sum here.

Private costs total: Use the same process used to calculate the Business costs total to determine the amount of operating costs that should be assigned to Private use.

How to log information in the Trips Log, Continued

Specifically, the **'Trips Details'** pages (example on page 21)

Trip No. Enter the number of the Trip to which the Details being added pertain. This will be the same number that was used for that Trip on the associated **Vehicle Use Log** page.

Purpose of Trip / Incidents Y / N Enter the reason that the Trip was made; this is particularly important for business trips. Also: write a 'Y' or 'N' to signify, yes or no, whether there were any incidents during the trip. Incidents could be technical problems, such as accidents, malfunctions, etc. Explain any 'Y' with an entry in the Technical Incidents Log.

Odometer Enter the odometer reading at the time of refueling, so that fuel use can be calculated accurately.

Distance Calculate the distance driven since the previous refueling, using the odometer reading recorded at that time.

Oil Added Enter the Amount of engine oil added and the Cost of purchasing that oil in the spaces provided.

Fuel Added Enter the Amount of fuel added and the Cost of purchasing that fuel in the spaces provided.

Other Expenses Enter the Cost and the name of the Item of any other expense related to using the car for that trip (e.g. tolls, car wash, etc). The costs of technical items, however, would normally be recorded in **Part 3**.

D / F Calculate and enter the fuel use since the previous refueling, using the **Distance** since last refueling and the Amount of **Fuel Added** that were recorded here. Express as MPG or Km/L, as appropriate.

Trip Details notes continue on the next page

The '**Trips Details**' pages, continued (example on page 21)

Totals this page:	Enter the sum of the entries made for each data type on the given page.
Totals brought forward:	Copy the '**Totals to Date**' from the previous **Trips Details** page and enter them here.
Totals to Date:	Enter the sums of the 'Totals this page' and the 'Totals brought forward' on the given page.
Total Cost:	Sum the totals of the **Oil Added**, **Fuel Added** and **Other Expenses** costs and enter this figure in the space provided. This represents the **Total Cost** of running your vehicle for the Trips listed on this page and the associated **Vehicle Use Log** page (maintenance costs are recorded in **Part 3**).
Information is accurate	The responsible person should sign on the line provided, to attest to the fact that the information entered on this page and the associated **Vehicle Use Log** page is accurate.

Units to be used in this book - by entering your units below it will not be necessary to label your entries on the Trips Log pages:

Odometer / Distances (e.g. miles, Km): ________

Fuel (e.g. gallons, litres): ________

Oil (e.g. quarts, litres): ________

Currency (e.g. USD, Euro): ________

Other: ______________________________ ________

Vehicle Use Log

Year: 2021

Trip No.	Date	Driver's Name / Signature	Trip		Odometer		Distance		
			From	To	Departure	Arrival	Business	Private	Total
1	3/29	J. Smith	Office	Post Office	76030	76039	9	-	9
2	3/29	J. Smith	Post Office	Home	76039	76049	-	10	10
3									
4									
5									
6									
7									
8									
9									
10									

Example **Vehicle Use Log** page:

On the 29th of March, 2021, J. Smith drove his vehicle from his office to the post office, a distance of 9 (miles or km, as appropriate), recorded as business travel. He then drove home and recorded that trip as private travel. Subsequent trips were made, some private and some business, and the page was filled with ten trips in all.

The total distance recorded for the trips on this page was 117 (miles or km); this value was entered below as the 'Totals this page.' The **Totals to Date** value from the PREVIOUS **Vehicle Use Log** page (3614 miles or km), was entered below as the 'Totals brought forward.' The present 'Totals this page' and 'Totals brought forward' values were then added together to get the present '**Totals to Date**.' This is the absolute total distance that the car has been driven so far, according to the record made by this book. Note that the business and private distances were also totaled, separately, and that they add together to give the absolute totals.

The % of Total distance driven that was for business, up to the present date, was calculated to be 2067 / 3731 = 0.55 = 55%
The % of Total distance driven that was private, up to the present date, was calculated to be 1664 / 3731 = 0.45 = 45%
Business costs total was calculated to be 55% of the **Total** Cost (545.30 - from the **Trips Details** page) = 300.00. This makes a running cost over the time up to date. Private costs total was calculated to be 245.30, using the same method.

The sums of the Business and Private distances driven must equal the **Total** distances recorded. Use the **Trips Details** page (below) to record more information (as necessary) about the Trips logged on this page. Make sure that the **Trip No.**s are identical on both pages, in order to be clear as to which Trip the Details refer.	% of **Total** distance driven that was for business:	% of **Total** distance driven that was private:	Calculate, using data from the **Trips Details** page: Business costs total:	Private costs total:		Business	Private	Total
					Totals this page:	57	60	117
					Totals brought forward:	2010	1604	3614
	55 %	45 %	300.00	245.30	**Totals to Date:**	2067	1664	3731

Trips Details

Trip No.	Purpose of Trip / Incidents Y/N (incidents could be accidents, malfunctions, etc - enter Y or N here. Explain on the corresponding Technical Incidents Log page, as required)	Odometer (at time of fuel or oil added)	Distance (since last refuel)	Oil Added		Fuel Added		Other Expenses (e.g. tolls)		D / F (Km/L or MPG)
				Amount	Cost	Amount	Cost	Cost	Item	
1	Collect company mail. N	76031	201	1	7.88	6.7	21.44	-	-	30
2	Drive home. N	-	-	-	-	-	-	-	-	-
3										
4										
5										
6										
7										
8										
9										
10										

Example **Trips Details** page:

J. Smith drove to the post office and then home on 29 March with no incidents encountered on either trip. The trip numbers on this page correspond to the trips entered in the corresponding **Vehicle Use Log** page. During Trip 1 J. Smith bought fuel and motor oil and noted the respective amounts and costs, using the units he has specified for this book and written on page 19.

In the 'Totals this page' row below, he has entered the total oil and fuel quantities added in the 10 trips recorded on this page and their respective total costs. He then took the '**Totals to Date**' figures from the PREVIOUS **Trips Details** page and wrote them in the spaces provided as 'Totals brought forward.' He summed the The 'Totals this page' and the 'Totals brought forward' values and entered them as the current '**Totals to Date**.'

From these current **Totals to Date** figures, the total **Oil Added** Cost (15.78), plus the total **Fuel Added** Cost (419.52) plus the total **Other Expenses** Cost (110.00) were then summed to give the overall **Total Cost** (545.30), all in the units specified for this book. This value represent the total recorded running cost for this vehicle (excluding maintenance costs, which are logged in Part 3). Add A + B + C to get **Total Cost**.

J. Smith, who is the responsible person for this vehicle, has signed the page to assert that all entries on this page and the associated **Vehicle Use Log** page are accurate.

	Oil Amount	Oil Cost	Fuel Amount	Fuel Cost	Other Expenses Cost	
Totals this page:	1	7.88	10.6	33.93	-	
Totals brought forward:	1	7.90	120.5	385.60	110.00	Total Cost:
Totals to Date:	2	15.78	131.1	419.52	110.0	545.30

The information recorded on this page and the page above are accurate. Signature:

J. Smith

VEHICLE USE LOG YEAR:

Trip No.	Date	Driver's Name / Signature	Trip		Odometer		Distance		
			From	To	Departure	Arrival	Business	Private	**Total**

The sums of the Business and Private distances driven must equal the **Total** distances recorded.

Use the **Trips Details** page (below) to record more information (as necessary) about the Trips logged on this page. Make sure that the **Trip No.**s are identical on both pages, in order to be clear as to which Trip the Details refer.

% of **Total** distance driven that was for business:	% of **Total** distance driven that was private:	Calculate, using data from the **Trips Details** page: Business costs total:	Private costs total:
_____%	_____%	_____	_____

	Business	Private	Total
Totals this page:			
Totals brought forward:			
Totals to Date:			

Trips Details

Trip No.	**Purpose of Trip / Incidents Y/N** (incidents could be accidents, malfunctions, etc - enter Y or N here. Explain on the corresponding Technical Incidents Log page, as required)	**Odometer** (at time of fuel or oil added)	**Distance** (since last refuel)	**Oil Added**		**Fuel Added**		**Other Expenses** (e.g. tolls)		**D / F** (Km/L or MPG)
				Amount	Cost	Amount	Cost	Cost	Item	

The information recorded on this page and the page above are accurate. Signature:

	Oil Amount	Oil Cost	Fuel Amount	Fuel Cost	Other Cost	
Totals this page:						
Totals brought forward:						**Total Cost:** (A+B+C)
Totals to Date:		A		B	C	

VEHICLE USE LOG YEAR:

Trip No.	Date	Driver's Name / Signature	Trip		Odometer		Distance		
			From	To	Departure	Arrival	Business	Private	**Total**

The sums of the Business and Private distances driven must equal the **Total** distances recorded. Use the **Trips Details** page (below) to record more information (as necessary) about the Trips logged on this page. Make sure that the **Trip No.**s are identical on both pages, in order to be clear as to which Trip the Details refer.	% of **Total** distance driven that was for business: ______%	% of **Total** distance driven that was private: ______%	Calculate, using data from the **Trips Details** page: Business costs total: ______	Private costs total: ______	Totals this page:			
					Totals brought forward:			
					Totals to Date:			

Trips Details

Trip No.	**Purpose of Trip / Incidents Y/N** (incidents could be accidents, malfunctions, etc - enter Y or N here. Explain on the corresponding Technical Incidents Log page, as required)	**Odometer** (at time of fuel or oil added)	**Distance** (since last refuel)	**Oil Added**		**Fuel Added**		**Other Expenses** (e.g. tolls)		**D / F** (Km/L or MPG)
				Amount	Cost	Amount	Cost	Cost	Item	

The information recorded on this page and the page above are accurate. Signature:

	Oil Amount	Oil Cost	Fuel Amount	Fuel Cost	Other Cost	
Totals this page:						
Totals brought forward:						**Total Cost:** (A+B+C)
Totals to Date:		A		B	C	

Vehicle Use Log — Year:

Trip No.	Date	Driver's Name / Signature	Trip		Odometer		Distance		
			From	To	Departure	Arrival	Business	Private	**Total**

The sums of the Business and Private distances driven must equal the **Total** distances recorded.

Use the **Trips Details** page (below) to record more information (as necessary) about the Trips logged on this page. Make sure that the **Trip No.**s are identical on both pages, in order to be clear as to which Trip the Details refer.

% of **Total** distance driven that was for business:	% of **Total** distance driven that was private:	Calculate, using data from the **Trips Details** page: Business costs total:	Private costs total:
______%	______%	______	______

	Business	Private	Total
Totals this page:			
Totals brought forward:			
Totals to Date:			

TRIPS DETAILS

Trip No.	Purpose of Trip / Incidents Y/N (incidents could be accidents, malfunctions, etc - enter Y or N here. Explain on the corresponding Technical Incidents Log page, as required)	Odometer (at time of fuel or oil added)	Distance (since last refuel)	Oil Added		Fuel Added		Other Expenses (e.g. tolls)		D / F (Km/L or MPG)
				Amount	Cost	Amount	Cost	Cost	Item	

	Oil Amount	Oil Cost	Fuel Amount	Fuel Cost	Other Cost	
Totals this page:						
Totals brought forward:						**Total Cost:** (A+B+C)
Totals to Date:		A		B	C	

The information recorded on this page and the page above are accurate. Signature:

____

Vehicle Use Log — Year:

Trip No.	Date	Driver's Name / Signature	Trip		Odometer		Distance		
			From	To	Departure	Arrival	Business	Private	**Total**

	% of **Total** distance driven that was for business:	% of **Total** distance driven that was private:	Calculate, using data from the **Trips Details** page: Business costs total:	Private costs total:		Business	Private	Total
The sums of the Business and Private distances driven must equal the **Total** distances recorded. Use the **Trips Details** page (below) to record more information (as necessary) about the Trips logged on this page. Make sure that the **Trip No.**s are identical on both pages, in order to be clear as to which Trip the Details refer.	______%	______%	________	________	Totals this page:			
					Totals brought forward:			
					Totals to Date:			

TRIPS DETAILS

Trip No.	**Purpose of Trip / Incidents Y/N** (Incidents could be accidents, malfunctions, etc - enter Y or N here. Explain on the corresponding Technical Incidents Log page, as required)	**Odometer** (at time of fuel or oil added)	**Distance** (since last refuel)	**Oil Added**		**Fuel Added**		**Other Expenses** (e.g. tolls)		**D / F** (Km/L or MPG)
				Amount	Cost	Amount	Cost	Cost	Item	
The information recorded on this page and the page above are accurate. Signature:		Totals this page:								
		Totals brought forward:							**Total Cost:** (A+B+C)	
		Totals to Date:			A		B	C		

Vehicle Use Log — Year:

Trip No.	Date	Driver's Name / Signature	Trip		Odometer		Distance		
			From	To	Departure	Arrival	Business	Private	**Total**

	% of **Total** distance driven that was for business:	% of **Total** distance driven that was private:	Calculate, using data from the **Trips Details** page: Business costs total:	Private costs total:				
The sums of the Business and Private distances driven must equal the **Total** distances recorded. Use the **Trips Details** page (below) to record more information (as necessary) about the Trips logged on this page. Make sure that the **Trip No.**s are identical on both pages, in order to be clear as to which Trip the Details refer.	______%	______%	________	________	Totals this page:			
					Totals brought forward:			
					Totals to Date:			

Trips Details

Trip No.	Purpose of Trip / Incidents Y/N (incidents could be accidents, malfunctions, etc - enter Y or N here. Explain on the corresponding Technical Incidents Log page, as required)	Odometer (at time of fuel or oil added)	Distance (since last refuel)	Oil Added		Fuel Added		Other Expenses (e.g. tolls)		D / F (Km/L or MPG)
				Amount	Cost	Amount	Cost	Cost	Item	
The information recorded on this page and the page above are accurate. Signature:			Totals this page:							
			Totals brought forward:						Total Cost: (A+B+C)	
			Totals to Date:		A		B	C		

VEHICLE USE LOG YEAR:

Trip No.	Date	Driver's Name / Signature	Trip		Odometer		Distance		
			From	To	Departure	Arrival	Business	Private	**Total**

The sums of the Business and Private distances driven must equal the **Total** distances recorded. Use the **Trips Details** page (below) to record more information (as necessary) about the Trips logged on this page. Make sure that the **Trip No.**s are identical on both pages, in order to be clear as to which Trip the Details refer.	% of **Total** distance driven that was for business: ______%	% of **Total** distance driven that was private: ______%	Calculate, using data from the **Trips Details** page: Business costs total: ______	Private costs total: ______	Totals this page:			
					Totals brought forward:			
					Totals to Date:			

TRIPS DETAILS

Trip No.	Purpose of Trip / Incidents Y/N (incidents could be accidents, malfunctions, etc - enter Y or N here. Explain on the corresponding Technical Incidents Log page, as required)	Odometer (at time of fuel or oil added)	Distance (since last refuel)	Oil Added		Fuel Added		Other Expenses (e.g. tolls)		D / F (Km/L or MPG)
				Amount	Cost	Amount	Cost	Cost	Item	

The information recorded on this page and the page above are accurate. Signature:								
	Totals this page:							
	Totals brought forward:						**Total Cost:** (A+B+C)	
	Totals to Date:		A		B	C		

Vehicle Use Log

Year:

Trip No.	**Date**	**Driver's Name / Signature**	**Trip**		**Odometer**		**Distance**		
			From	To	Departure	Arrival	Business	Private	**Total**

The sums of the Business and Private distances driven must equal the **Total** distances recorded.

Use the **Trips Details** page (below) to record more information (as necessary) about the Trips logged on this page. Make sure that the **Trip No.**s are identical on both pages, in order to be clear as to which Trip the Details refer.

% of **Total** distance driven that was for business:	% of **Total** distance driven that was private:	Calculate, using data from the **Trips Details** page: Business costs total:	Private costs total:
_____%	_____%	_____	_____

	Business	Private	**Total**
Totals this page:			
Totals brought forward:			
Totals to Date:			

TRIPS DETAILS

Trip No.	Purpose of Trip / Incidents Y/N (incidents could be accidents, malfunctions, etc - enter Y or N here. Explain on the corresponding Technical Incidents Log page, as required)	Odometer (at time of fuel or oil added)	Distance (since last refuel)	Oil Added		Fuel Added		Other Expenses (e.g. tolls)		D / F (Km/L or MPG)
				Amount	Cost	Amount	Cost	Cost	Item	
The information recorded on this page and the page above are accurate. Signature:		Totals this page:								
		Totals brought forward:							**Total Cost:** (A+B+C)	
		Totals to Date:			A		B	C		

VEHICLE USE LOG

YEAR:

Trip No.	Date	Driver's Name / Signature	Trip		Odometer		Distance		
			From	To	Departure	Arrival	Business	Private	**Total**

The sums of the Business and Private distances driven must equal the **Total** distances recorded. Use the **Trips Details** page (below) to record more information (as necessary) about the Trips logged on this page. Make sure that the **Trip No.**s are identical on both pages, in order to be clear as to which Trip the Details refer.	% of **Total** distance driven that was for business: _____%	% of **Total** distance driven that was private: _____%	Calculate, using data from the **Trips Details** page: Business costs total: _____	Private costs total: _____	Totals this page:			
					Totals brought forward:			
					Totals to Date:			

Trips Details

Trip No.	Purpose of Trip / Incidents Y/N (incidents could be accidents, malfunctions, etc - enter Y or N here. Explain on the corresponding Technical Incidents Log page, as required)	Odometer (at time of fuel or oil added)	Distance (since last refuel)	Oil Added		Fuel Added		Other Expenses (e.g. tolls)		D / F (Km/L or MPG)
				Amount	Cost	Amount	Cost	Cost	Item	

The information recorded on this page and the page above are accurate. Signature:

____

	Oil Amount	Oil Cost	Fuel Amount	Fuel Cost	Other Cost	
Totals this page:						
Totals brought forward:						**Total Cost:** (A+B+C)
Totals to Date:		A		B	C	

Vehicle Use Log Year:

Trip No.	Date	Driver's Name / Signature	Trip		Odometer		Distance		
			From	To	Departure	Arrival	Business	Private	**Total**
The sums of the Business and Private distances driven must equal the **Total** distances recorded. Use the **Trips Details** page (below) to record more information (as necessary) about the Trips logged on this page. Make sure that the **Trip No.**s are identical on both pages, in order to be clear as to which Trip the Details refer.			% of **Total** distance driven that was for business: ______%	% of **Total** distance driven that was private: ______%	Calculate, using data from the **Trips Details** page: Business costs total: ______ Private costs total: ______	Totals this page:			
						Totals brought forward:			
						Totals to Date:			

Trips Details

Trip No.	Purpose of Trip / Incidents Y/N (incidents could be accidents, malfunctions, etc - enter Y or N here. Explain on the corresponding Technical Incidents Log page, as required)	Odometer (at time of fuel or oil added)	Distance (since last refuel)	Oil Added		Fuel Added		Other Expenses (e.g. tolls)		D / F (Km/L or MPG)
				Amount	Cost	Amount	Cost	Cost	Item	

	Oil Amount	Oil Cost	Fuel Amount	Fuel Cost	Other Expenses Cost	
Totals this page:						
Totals brought forward:						**Total Cost:** (A+B+C)
Totals to Date:		A		B	C	

The information recorded on this page and the page above are accurate. Signature:

____

VEHICLE USE LOG YEAR:

Trip No.	Date	Driver's Name / Signature	Trip		Odometer		Distance		
			From	To	Departure	Arrival	Business	Private	**Total**

The sums of the Business and Private distances driven must equal the **Total** distances recorded. Use the **Trips Details** page (below) to record more information (as necessary) about the Trips logged on this page. Make sure that the **Trip No.**s are identical on both pages, in order to be clear as to which Trip the Details refer.	% of **Total** distance driven that was for business: ______%	% of **Total** distance driven that was private: ______%	Calculate, using data from the **Trips Details** page: Business costs total: ________	Private costs total: ________	Totals this page:			
					Totals brought forward:			
					Totals to Date:			

TRIPS DETAILS

Trip No.	Purpose of Trip / Incidents Y/N (incidents could be accidents, malfunctions, etc enter Y or N here. Explain on the corresponding Technical Incidents Log page, as required)	Odometer (at time of fuel or oil added)	Distance (since last refuel)	Oil Added		Fuel Added		Other Expenses (e.g. tolls)		D / F (Km/L or MPG)
				Amount	Cost	Amount	Cost	Cost	Item	

The information recorded on this page and the page above are accurate. Signature:							
	Totals this page:						
	Totals brought forward:						**Total Cost:** (A+B+C)
	Totals to Date:		A		B	C	

VEHICLE USE LOG YEAR:

Trip No.	Date	Driver's Name / Signature	Trip		Odometer		Distance		
			From	To	Departure	Arrival	Business	Private	**Total**

The sums of the Business and Private distances driven must equal the **Total** distances recorded.

Use the **Trips Details** page (below) to record more information (as necessary) about the Trips logged on this page. Make sure that the **Trip No.**s are identical on both pages, in order to be clear as to which Trip the Details refer.

% of **Total** distance driven that was for business:	% of **Total** distance driven that was private:	Calculate, using data from the **Trips Details** page: Business costs total:	Private costs total:
______%	______%	________	________

	Business	Private	Total
Totals this page:			
Totals brought forward:			
Totals to Date:			

Trips Details

Trip No.	**Purpose of Trip / Incidents Y/N** (incidents could be accidents, malfunctions, etc - enter Y or N here. Explain on the corresponding Technical Incidents Log page, as required)	**Odometer** (at time of fuel or oil added)	**Distance** (since last refuel)	**Oil Added**		**Fuel Added**		**Other Expenses** (e.g. tolls)		**D / F** (Km/L or MPG)
				Amount	Cost	Amount	Cost	Cost	Item	
The information recorded on this page and the page above are accurate. Signature:		Totals this page:								
		Totals brought forward:							**Total Cost:** (A+B+C)	
		Totals to Date:			A		B	C		

Vehicle Use Log   Year:

Trip No.	Date	Driver's Name / Signature	Trip		Odometer		Distance		
			From	To	Departure	Arrival	Business	Private	**Total**

The sums of the Business and Private distances driven must equal the **Total** distances recorded. Use the **Trips Details** page (below) to record more information (as necessary) about the Trips logged on this page. Make sure that the **Trip No.**s are identical on both pages, in order to be clear as to which Trip the Details refer.	% of **Total** distance driven that was for business: _____%	% of **Total** distance driven that was private: _____%	Calculate, using data from the **Trips Details** page: Business costs total: _____	Private costs total: _____	Totals this page:		
					Totals brought forward:		
					Totals to Date:		

TRIPS DETAILS

Trip No.	Purpose of Trip / Incidents Y/N (incidents could be accidents, malfunctions, etc - enter Y or N here. Explain on the corresponding Technical Incidents Log page, as required)	Odometer (at time of fuel or oil added)	Distance (since last refuel)	Oil Added		Fuel Added		Other Expenses (e.g. tolls)		D / F (Km/L or MPG)
				Amount	Cost	Amount	Cost	Cost	Item	

The information recorded on this page and the page above are accurate. Signature:							
	Totals this page:						
	Totals brought forward:						**Total Cost:** (A+B+C)
	Totals to Date:		A		B	C	

VEHICLE USE LOG YEAR:

Trip No.	Date	Driver's Name / Signature	Trip		Odometer		Distance		
			From	To	Departure	Arrival	Business	Private	**Total**

The sums of the Business and Private distances driven must equal the **Total** distances recorded. Use the **Trips Details** page (below) to record more information (as necessary) about the Trips logged on this page. Make sure that the **Trip No.**s are identical on both pages, in order to be clear as to which Trip the Details refer.	% of **Total** distance driven that was for business: ______%	% of **Total** distance driven that was private: ______%	Calculate, using data from the **Trips Details** page: Business costs total: ______	Private costs total: ______	Totals this page:			
					Totals brought forward:			
					Totals to Date:			

Trips Details

Trip No.	Purpose of Trip / Incidents Y/N (incidents could be accidents, malfunctions, etc - enter Y or N here. Explain on the corresponding Technical Incidents Log page, as required)	Odometer (at time of fuel or oil added)	Distance (since last refuel)	Oil Added		Fuel Added		Other Expenses (e.g. tolls)		D / F (Km/L or MPG)
				Amount	Cost	Amount	Cost	Cost	Item	
The information recorded on this page and the page above are accurate. Signature:			Totals this page:							
			Totals brought forward:						Total Cost: (A+B+C)	
			Totals to Date:		A		B	C		

VEHICLE USE LOG YEAR:

Trip No.	Date	Driver's Name / Signature	**Trip**		**Odometer**		**Distance**		
			From	To	Departure	Arrival	Business	Private	**Total**

The sums of the Business and Private distances driven must equal the **Total** distances recorded. Use the **Trips Details** page (below) to record more information (as necessary) about the Trips logged on this page. Make sure that the **Trip No.**s are identical on both pages, in order to be clear as to which Trip the Details refer.	% of **Total** distance driven that was for business: _______%	% of **Total** distance driven that was private: _______%	Calculate, using data from the **Trips Details** page: Business costs total: _______	Private costs total: _______	Totals this page:			
					Totals brought forward:			
					Totals to Date:			

TRIPS DETAILS

Trip No.	Purpose of Trip / Incidents Y/N (incidents could be accidents, malfunctions, etc - enter Y or N here. Explain on the corresponding Technical Incidents Log page, as required)	Odometer (at time of fuel or oil added)	Distance (since last refuel)	Oil Added		Fuel Added		Other Expenses (e.g. tolls)		D / F (Km/L or MPG)
				Amount	Cost	Amount	Cost	Cost	Item	

The information recorded on this page and the page above are accurate. Signature:

____

	Oil Amount	Oil Cost	Fuel Amount	Fuel Cost	Other Cost	
Totals this page:						
Totals brought forward:						**Total Cost:** (A+B+C)
Totals to Date:		A		B	C	

Vehicle Use Log — Year:

Trip No.	Date	Driver's Name / Signature	Trip		Odometer		Distance		
			From	To	Departure	Arrival	Business	Private	**Total**

The sums of the Business and Private distances driven must equal the **Total** distances recorded. Use the **Trips Details** page (below) to record more information (as necessary) about the Trips logged on this page. Make sure that the **Trip No.**s are identical on both pages, in order to be clear as to which Trip the Details refer.	% of **Total** distance driven that was for business: _______%	% of **Total** distance driven that was private: _______%	Calculate, using data from the **Trips Details** page: Business costs total: _______	Private costs total: _______	Totals this page:			
					Totals brought forward:			
					Totals to Date:			

TRIPS DETAILS

Trip No.	Purpose of Trip / Incidents Y/N (incidents could be accidents, malfunctions, etc - enter Y or N here. Explain on the corresponding Technical Incidents Log page, as required)	Odometer (at time of fuel or oil added)	Distance (since last refuel)	Oil Added		Fuel Added		Other Expenses (e.g. tolls)		D / F (Km/L or MPG)
				Amount	Cost	Amount	Cost	Cost	Item	
The information recorded on this page and the page above are accurate. Signature:		Totals this page:								
		Totals brought forward:							**Total Cost:** (A+B+C)	
		Totals to Date:			A		B	C		

VEHICLE USE LOG YEAR:

Trip No.	Date	Driver's Name / Signature	Trip		Odometer		Distance		
			From	To	Departure	Arrival	Business	Private	**Total**

The sums of the Business and Private distances driven must equal the **Total** distances recorded. Use the **Trips Details** page (below) to record more information (as necessary) about the Trips logged on this page. Make sure that the **Trip No.**s are identical on both pages, in order to be clear as to which Trip the Details refer.	% of **Total** distance driven that was for business: ______%	% of **Total** distance driven that was private: ______%	Calculate, using data from the **Trips Details** page: Business costs total: ______	Private costs total: ______			
					Totals this page:		
					Totals brought forward:		
					Totals to Date:		

Trips Details

Trip No.	Purpose of Trip / Incidents Y/N (incidents could be accidents, malfunctions, etc - enter Y or N here. Explain on the corresponding Technical Incidents Log page, as required)	Odometer (at time of fuel or oil added)	Distance (since last refuel)	Oil Added		Fuel Added		Other Expenses (e.g. tolls)		D / F (Km/L or MPG)
				Amount	Cost	Amount	Cost	Cost	Item	

The information recorded on this page and the page above are accurate. Signature:

____

	Oil Amount	Oil Cost	Fuel Amount	Fuel Cost	Other Cost	
Totals this page:						
Totals brought forward:						**Total Cost:** (A+B+C)
Totals to Date:		A		B	C	

Vehicle Use Log   Year:

Trip No.	Date	Driver's Name / Signature	Trip		Odometer		Distance		
			From	To	Departure	Arrival	Business	Private	**Total**

The sums of the Business and Private distances driven must equal the **Total** distances recorded. Use the **Trips Details** page (below) to record more information (as necessary) about the Trips logged on this page. Make sure that the **Trip No.**s are identical on both pages, in order to be clear as to which Trip the Details refer.	% of **Total** distance driven that was for business: ______%	% of **Total** distance driven that was private: ______%	Calculate, using data from the **Trips Details** page: Business costs total: ________ Private costs total: ________	Totals this page: Totals brought forward: **Totals to Date:**			

TRIPS DETAILS

Trip No.	Purpose of Trip / Incidents Y/N (incidents could be accidents, malfunctions, etc - enter Y or N here. Explain on the corresponding Technical Incidents Log page, as required)	Odometer (at time of fuel or oil added)	Distance (since last refuel)	Oil Added		Fuel Added		Other Expenses (e.g. tolls)		D / F (Km/L or MPG)
				Amount	Cost	Amount	Cost	Cost	Item	

The information recorded on this page and the page above are accurate. Signature:

	Oil Amount	Oil Cost	Fuel Amount	Fuel Cost	Other Cost	
Totals this page:						
Totals brought forward:						**Total Cost:** (A+B+C)
Totals to Date:		A		B	C	

Trips Details

Trip No.	Purpose of Trip / Incidents Y/N (incidents could be accidents, malfunctions, etc - enter Y or N here. Explain on the corresponding Technical Incidents Log page, as required)	Odometer (at time of fuel or oil added)	Distance (since last refuel)	Oil Added		Fuel Added		Other Expenses (e.g. tolls)		D / F (Km/L or MPG)
				Amount	Cost	Amount	Cost	Cost	Item	
The information recorded on this page and the page above are accurate. Signature:		Totals this page:								
		Totals brought forward:							Total Cost: (A+B+C)	
		Totals to Date:			A		B	C		

VEHICLE USE LOG   YEAR:

Trip No.	Date	Driver's Name / Signature	Trip		Odometer		Distance		
			From	To	Departure	Arrival	Business	Private	**Total**

The sums of the Business and Private distances driven must equal the **Total** distances recorded.

Use the **Trips Details** page (below) to record more information (as necessary) about the Trips logged on this page. Make sure that the **Trip No.**s are identical on both pages, in order to be clear as to which Trip the Details refer.

% of **Total** distance driven that was for business: ______%

% of **Total** distance driven that was private: ______%

Calculate, using data from the **Trips Details** page:

Business costs total: ________

Private costs total: ________

	Business	Private	Total
Totals this page:			
Totals brought forward:			
Totals to Date:			

VEHICLE USE LOG YEAR:

Trip No.	Date	Driver's Name / Signature	Trip		Odometer		Distance		
			From	To	Departure	Arrival	Business	Private	**Total**

The sums of the Business and Private distances driven must equal the **Total** distances recorded. Use the **Trips Details** page (below) to record more information (as necessary) about the Trips logged on this page. Make sure that the **Trip No.**s are identical on both pages, in order to be clear as to which Trip the Details refer.	% of **Total** distance driven that was for business: ______%	% of **Total** distance driven that was private: ______%	Calculate, using data from the **Trips Details** page: Business costs total: ________	Private costs total: ________	Totals this page:			
					Totals brought forward:			
					Totals to Date:			

Trips Details

Trip No.	Purpose of Trip / Incidents Y/N (incidents could be accidents, malfunctions, etc - enter Y or N here. Explain on the corresponding Technical Incidents Log page, as required)	Odometer (at time of fuel or oil added)	Distance (since last refuel)	Oil Added		Fuel Added		Other Expenses (e.g. tolls)		D / F (Km/L or MPG)
				Amount	Cost	Amount	Cost	Cost	Item	
The information recorded on this page and the page above are accurate. Signature:		Totals this page:								
		Totals brought forward:							Total Cost: (A+B+C)	
		Totals to Date:			A		B	C		

Vehicle Use Log — Year:

Trip No.	Date	Driver's Name / Signature	Trip		Odometer		Distance		
			From	To	Departure	Arrival	Business	Private	**Total**

The sums of the Business and Private distances driven must equal the **Total** distances recorded. Use the **Trips Details** page (below) to record more information (as necessary) about the Trips logged on this page. Make sure that the **Trip No.**s are identical on both pages, in order to be clear as to which Trip the Details refer.	% of **Total** distance driven that was for business: _____%	% of **Total** distance driven that was private: _____%	Calculate, using data from the **Trips Details** page: Business costs total: _____	Private costs total: _____	Totals this page:			
					Totals brought forward:			
					Totals to Date:			

Trips Details

Trip No.	Purpose of Trip / Incidents Y/N (incidents could be accidents, malfunctions, etc enter Y or N here. Explain on the corresponding Technical Incidents Log page, as required)	Odometer (at time of fuel or oil added)	Distance (since last refuel)	Oil Added		Fuel Added		Other Expenses (e.g. tolls)		D / F (Km/L or MPG)
				Amount	Cost	Amount	Cost	Cost	Item	
The information recorded on this page and the page above are accurate. Signature:		Totals this page:								
		Totals brought forward:							Total Cost: (A+B+C)	
		Totals to Date:			A		B	C		

Vehicle Use Log   Year:

Trip No.	Date	Driver's Name / Signature	Trip		Odometer		Distance		
			From	To	Departure	Arrival	Business	Private	**Total**

Notes	% of **Total** distance driven that was for business:	% of **Total** distance driven that was private:	Business costs total:	Private costs total:		Business	Private	Total
The sums of the Business and Private distances driven must equal the **Total** distances recorded. Use the **Trips Details** page (below) to record more information (as necessary) about the Trips logged on this page. Make sure that the **Trip No.**s are identical on both pages, in order to be clear as to which Trip the Details refer.	______%	______%	______	______	Totals this page:			
					Totals brought forward:			
					Totals to Date:			

Calculate, using data from the **Trips Details** page: Business costs total / Private costs total.

TRIPS DETAILS

Trip No.	Purpose of Trip / Incidents Y/N (incidents could be accidents, malfunctions, etc - enter Y or N here. Explain on the corresponding Technical Incidents Log page, as required)	Odometer (at time of fuel or oil added)	Distance (since last refuel)	Oil Added		Fuel Added		Other Expenses (e.g. tolls)		D / F (Km/L or MPG)
				Amount	Cost	Amount	Cost	Cost	Item	

		Oil Amount	Oil Cost	Fuel Amount	Fuel Cost	Other Cost	
The information recorded on this page and the page above are accurate. Signature:	Totals this page:						
	Totals brought forward:						**Total Cost:** (A+B+C)
	Totals to Date:		A		B	C	

Vehicle Use Log							Year:		
Trip No.	**Date**	**Driver's Name / Signature**	**Trip**		**Odometer**		**Distance**		
			From	To	Departure	Arrival	Business	Private	**Total**

The sums of the Business and Private distances driven must equal the **Total** distances recorded. Use the **Trips Details** page (below) to record more information (as necessary) about the Trips logged on this page. Make sure that the **Trip No.**s are identical on both pages, in order to be clear as to which Trip the Details refer.	% of **Total** distance driven that was for business: _____%	% of **Total** distance driven that was private: _____%	Calculate, using data from the **Trips Details** page: Business costs total: _____	Private costs total: _____	Totals this page:			
					Totals brought forward:			
					Totals to Date:			

Trips Details

Trip No.	**Purpose of Trip / Incidents Y/N** (incidents could be accidents, malfunctions, etc - enter Y or N here. Explain on the corresponding Technical Incidents Log page, as required)	**Odometer** (at time of fuel or oil added)	**Distance** (since last refuel)	**Oil Added**		**Fuel Added**		**Other Expenses** (e.g. tolls)		**D / F** (Km/L or MPG)
				Amount	Cost	Amount	Cost	Cost	Item	

The information recorded on this page and the page above are accurate. Signature:

	Oil Amount	Oil Cost	Fuel Amount	Fuel Cost	Other Cost	
Totals this page:						
Totals brought forward:						**Total Cost:** (A+B+C)
Totals to Date:		A		B	C	

VEHICLE USE LOG YEAR:

Trip No.	Date	Driver's Name / Signature	Trip		Odometer		Distance		
			From	To	Departure	Arrival	Business	Private	**Total**

The sums of the Business and Private distances driven must equal the **Total** distances recorded. Use the **Trips Details** page (below) to record more information (as necessary) about the Trips logged on this page. Make sure that the **Trip No.**s are identical on both pages, in order to be clear as to which Trip the Details refer.	% of **Total** distance driven that was for business: ______%	% of **Total** distance driven that was private: ______%	Calculate, using data from the **Trips Details** page: Business costs total: ______	Private costs total: ______	Totals this page:			
					Totals brought forward:			
					Totals to Date:			

Trips Details

Trip No.	Purpose of Trip / Incidents Y/N (incidents could be accidents, malfunctions, etc - enter Y or N here. Explain on the corresponding Technical Incidents Log page, as required)	Odometer (at time of fuel or oil added)	Distance (since last refuel)	Oil Added		Fuel Added		Other Expenses (e.g. tolls)		D / F (Km/L or MPG)
				Amount	Cost	Amount	Cost	Cost	Item	

The information recorded on this page and the page above are accurate. Signature:

____

	Oil Amount	Oil Cost	Fuel Amount	Fuel Cost	Other Cost	
Totals this page:						
Totals brought forward:						**Total Cost:** (A+B+C)
Totals to Date:		A		B	C	

Vehicle Use Log — Year:

Trip No.	Date	Driver's Name / Signature	Trip		Odometer		Distance		
			From	To	Departure	Arrival	Business	Private	**Total**

The sums of the Business and Private distances driven must equal the **Total** distances recorded. Use the **Trips Details** page (below) to record more information (as necessary) about the Trips logged on this page. Make sure that the **Trip No.**s are identical on both pages, in order to be clear as to which Trip the Details refer.	% of **Total** distance driven that was for business: ______%	% of **Total** distance driven that was private: ______%	Calculate, using data from the **Trips Details** page: Business costs total: ______	Private costs total: ______	Totals this page:		
					Totals brought forward:		
					Totals to Date:		

TRIPS DETAILS											
Trip No.	**Purpose of Trip / Incidents Y/N** (incidents could be accidents, malfunctions, etc - enter Y or N here. Explain on the corresponding Technical Incidents Log page, as required)	**Odometer** (at time of fuel or oil added)	**Distance** (since last refuel)	**Oil Added**		**Fuel Added**		**Other Expenses** (e.g. tolls)		**D / F** (Km/L or MPG)
				Amount	Cost	Amount	Cost	Cost	Item	
The information recorded on this page and the page above are accurate. Signature:		Totals this page:								
		Totals brought forward:							**Total Cost:** (A+B+C)	
		Totals to Date:			A		B	C		

Vehicle Use Log   Year:

Trip No.	Date	Driver's Name / Signature	Trip		Odometer		Distance		
			From	To	Departure	Arrival	Business	Private	**Total**

The sums of the Business and Private distances driven must equal the **Total** distances recorded. Use the **Trips Details** page (below) to record more information (as necessary) about the Trips logged on this page. Make sure that the **Trip No.**s are identical on both pages, in order to be clear as to which Trip the Details refer.	% of **Total** distance driven that was for business: _______%	% of **Total** distance driven that was private: _______%	Calculate, using data from the **Trips Details** page: Business costs total: _________	Private costs total: _________	Totals this page:			
					Totals brought forward:			
					Totals to Date:			

Trips Details

Trip No.	**Purpose of Trip / Incidents Y/N** (incidents could be accidents, malfunctions, etc - enter Y or N here. Explain on the corresponding Technical Incidents Log page, as required)	**Odometer** (at time of fuel or oil added)	**Distance** (since last refuel)	**Oil Added**		**Fuel Added**		**Other Expenses** (e.g. tolls)		**D / F** (Km/L or MPG)
				Amount	Cost	Amount	Cost	Cost	Item	
The information recorded on this page and the page above are accurate. Signature:			Totals this page:							
			Totals brought forward:						**Total Cost:** (A+B+C)	
			Totals to Date:		A		B	C		

VEHICLE USE LOG   YEAR:

Trip No.	Date	Driver's Name / Signature	Trip		Odometer		Distance		
			From	To	Departure	Arrival	Business	Private	**Total**

Notes	% of **Total** distance driven that was for business:	% of **Total** distance driven that was private:	Calculate, using data from the **Trips Details** page: Business costs total:	Private costs total:		Business	Private	Total
The sums of the Business and Private distances driven must equal the **Total** distances recorded. Use the **Trips Details** page (below) to record more information (as necessary) about the Trips logged on this page. Make sure that the **Trip No.**s are identical on both pages, in order to be clear as to which Trip the Details refer.	______%	______%	______	______	Totals this page:			
					Totals brought forward:			
					Totals to Date:			

Trips Details

Trip No.	Purpose of Trip / Incidents Y/N (incidents could be accidents, malfunctions, etc - enter Y or N here. Explain on the corresponding Technical Incidents Log page, as required)	Odometer (at time of fuel or oil added)	Distance (since last refuel)	Oil Added		Fuel Added		Other Expenses (e.g. tolls)		D / F (Km/L or MPG)
				Amount	Cost	Amount	Cost	Cost	Item	

The information recorded on this page and the page above are accurate. Signature:							
	Totals this page:						
	Totals brought forward:						Total Cost: (A+B+C)
	Totals to Date:		A		B	C	

Vehicle Use Log

Year:

Trip No.	Date	Driver's Name / Signature	Trip		Odometer		Distance		
			From	To	Departure	Arrival	Business	Private	**Total**

The sums of the Business and Private distances driven must equal the **Total** distances recorded. Use the **Trips Details** page (below) to record more information (as necessary) about the Trips logged on this page. Make sure that the **Trip No.**s are identical on both pages, in order to be clear as to which Trip the Details refer.	% of **Total** distance driven that was for business: ______%	% of **Total** distance driven that was private: ______%	Calculate, using data from the **Trips Details** page: Business costs total: ______ Private costs total: ______	Totals this page:			
				Totals brought forward:			
				Totals to Date:			

TRIPS DETAILS

Trip No.	Purpose of Trip / Incidents Y/N (incidents could be accidents, malfunctions, etc - enter Y or N here. Explain on the corresponding Technical Incidents Log page, as required)	Odometer (at time of fuel or oil added)	Distance (since last refuel)	Oil Added		Fuel Added		Other Expenses (e.g. tolls)		D / F (Km/L or MPG)
				Amount	Cost	Amount	Cost	Cost	Item	

The information recorded on this page and the page above are accurate. Signature:								
	Totals this page:							
	Totals brought forward:							**Total Cost:** (A+B+C)
_______________	**Totals to Date:**		A		B	C		

Vehicle Use Log — Year:

Trip No.	Date	Driver's Name / Signature	Trip		Odometer		Distance		
			From	To	Departure	Arrival	Business	Private	**Total**

	% of **Total** distance driven that was for business:	% of **Total** distance driven that was private:	Calculate, using data from the **Trips Details** page: Business costs total:	Private costs total:		Business	Private	Total
The sums of the Business and Private distances driven must equal the **Total** distances recorded. Use the **Trips Details** page (below) to record more information (as necessary) about the Trips logged on this page. Make sure that the **Trip No.**s are identical on both pages, in order to be clear as to which Trip the Details refer.	______%	______%	________	________	Totals this page:			
					Totals brought forward:			
					Totals to Date:			

Trips Details

Trip No.	Purpose of Trip / Incidents Y/N (incidents could be accidents, malfunctions, etc - enter Y or N here. Explain on the corresponding Technical Incidents Log page, as required)	Odometer (at time of fuel or oil added)	Distance (since last refuel)	Oil Added		Fuel Added		Other Expenses (e.g. tolls)		D / F (Km/L or MPG)
				Amount	Cost	Amount	Cost	Cost	Item	

The information recorded on this page and the page above are accurate. Signature:		Oil Amount	Oil Cost	Fuel Amount	Fuel Cost	Other Cost	
	Totals this page:						
	Totals brought forward:						**Total Cost:** (A+B+C)
	Totals to Date:		A		B	C	

Vehicle Use Log — Year:

Trip No.	Date	Driver's Name / Signature	Trip		Odometer		Distance		
			From	To	Departure	Arrival	Business	Private	**Total**

The sums of the Business and Private distances driven must equal the **Total** distances recorded.

Use the **Trips Details** page (below) to record more information (as necessary) about the Trips logged on this page. Make sure that the **Trip No.**s are identical on both pages, in order to be clear as to which Trip the Details refer.

% of **Total** distance driven that was for business:	% of **Total** distance driven that was private:	Calculate, using data from the **Trips Details** page: Business costs total:	Private costs total:
______%	______%	______	______

	Business	Private	Total
Totals this page:			
Totals brought forward:			
Totals to Date:			

TRIPS DETAILS

Trip No.	Purpose of Trip / Incidents Y/N (Incidents could be accidents, malfunctions, etc - enter Y or N here. Explain on the corresponding Technical Incidents Log page, as required)	Odometer (at time of fuel or oil added)	Distance (since last refuel)	Oil Added		Fuel Added		Other Expenses (e.g. tolls)		D / F (Km/L or MPG)
				Amount	Cost	Amount	Cost	Cost	Item	

The information recorded on this page and the page above are accurate. Signature:		Oil Amount	Oil Cost	Fuel Amount	Fuel Cost	Other Cost	
	Totals this page:						
	Totals brought forward:						**Total Cost:** (A+B+C)
	Totals to Date:		A		B	C	

VEHICLE USE LOG YEAR:

Trip No.	Date	Driver's Name / Signature	Trip		Odometer		Distance		
			From	To	Departure	Arrival	Business	Private	**Total**

The sums of the Business and Private distances driven must equal the **Total** distances recorded.

Use the **Trips Details** page (below) to record more information (as necessary) about the Trips logged on this page. Make sure that the **Trip No.**s are identical on both pages, in order to be clear as to which Trip the Details refer.

% of **Total** distance driven that was for business:	% of **Total** distance driven that was private:	Calculate, using data from the **Trips Details** page: Business costs total:	Private costs total:
______%	______%	________	________

	Business	Private	Total
Totals this page:			
Totals brought forward:			
Totals to Date:			

TRIPS DETAILS

Trip No.	Purpose of Trip / Incidents Y/N (incidents could be accidents, malfunctions, etc - enter Y or N here. Explain on the corresponding Technical Incidents Log page, as required)	Odometer (at time of fuel or oil added)	Distance (since last refuel)	Oil Added		Fuel Added		Other Expenses (e.g. tolls)		D / F (Km/L or MPG)
				Amount	Cost	Amount	Cost	Cost	Item	

The information recorded on this page and the page above are accurate. Signature:							
	Totals this page:						
	Totals brought forward:						**Total Cost:** (A+B+C)
	Totals to Date:		A		B	C	

VEHICLE USE LOG YEAR:

Trip No.	Date	Driver's Name / Signature	Trip		Odometer		Distance		
			From	To	Departure	Arrival	Business	Private	**Total**

The sums of the Business and Private distances driven must equal the **Total** distances recorded. Use the **Trips Details** page (below) to record more information (as necessary) about the Trips logged on this page. Make sure that the **Trip No.**s are identical on both pages, in order to be clear as to which Trip the Details refer.	% of **Total** distance driven that was for business: ______%	% of **Total** distance driven that was private: ______%	Calculate, using data from the **Trips Details** page: Business costs total: ______	Private costs total: ______	Totals this page:			
					Totals brought forward:			
					Totals to Date:			

Trips Details

Trip No.	**Purpose of Trip / Incidents Y/N** (incidents could be accidents, malfunctions, etc - enter Y or N here. Explain on the corresponding Technical Incidents Log page, as required)	**Odometer** (at time of fuel or oil added)	**Distance** (since last refuel)	**Oil Added**		**Fuel Added**		**Other Expenses** (e.g. tolls)		**D / F** (Km/L or MPG)
				Amount	Cost	Amount	Cost	Cost	Item	

The information recorded on this page and the page above are accurate. Signature:		Oil Amount	Oil Cost	Fuel Amount	Fuel Cost	Other Cost	
	Totals this page:						
	Totals brought forward:						**Total Cost:** (A+B+C)
	Totals to Date:		A		B	C	

Vehicle Use Log							Year:		
Trip No.	Date	Driver's Name / Signature	Trip		Odometer		Distance		
			From	To	Departure	Arrival	Business	Private	**Total**

The sums of the Business and Private distances driven must equal the **Total** distances recorded. Use the **Trips Details** page (below) to record more information (as necessary) about the Trips logged on this page. Make sure that the **Trip No.**s are identical on both pages, in order to be clear as to which Trip the Details refer.	% of **Total** distance driven that was for business: _______%	% of **Total** distance driven that was private: _______%	Calculate, using data from the **Trips Details** page: Business costs total: _________	Private costs total: _________	Totals this page:			
					Totals brought forward:			
					Totals to Date:			

Trips Details

Trip No.	Purpose of Trip / Incidents Y/N (incidents could be accidents, malfunctions, etc enter Y or N here. Explain on the corresponding Technical Incidents Log page, as required)	Odometer (at time of fuel or oil added)	Distance (since last refuel)	Oil Added		Fuel Added		Other Expenses (e.g. tolls)		D / F (Km/L or MPG)
				Amount	Cost	Amount	Cost	Cost	Item	

The information recorded on this page and the page above are accurate. Signature:

	Oil Amount	Oil Cost	Fuel Amount	Fuel Cost	Other Cost	
Totals this page:						
Totals brought forward:						**Total Cost:** (A+B+C)
Totals to Date:		A		B	C	

Vehicle Use Log — Year:

Trip No.	Date	Driver's Name / Signature	Trip		Odometer		Distance		
			From	To	Departure	Arrival	Business	Private	**Total**

The sums of the Business and Private distances driven must equal the **Total** distances recorded.

Use the **Trips Details** page (below) to record more information (as necessary) about the Trips logged on this page. Make sure that the **Trip No.**s are identical on both pages, in order to be clear as to which Trip the Details refer.

% of **Total** distance driven that was for business:	% of **Total** distance driven that was private:	Calculate, using data from the **Trips Details** page: Business costs total:	Private costs total:
______%	______%	______	______

	Business	Private	Total
Totals this page:			
Totals brought forward:			
Totals to Date:			

Trips Details

Trip No.	Purpose of Trip / Incidents Y/N (incidents could be accidents, malfunctions, etc - enter Y or N here. Explain on the corresponding Technical Incidents Log page, as required)	Odometer (at time of fuel or oil added)	Distance (since last refuel)	Oil Added		Fuel Added		Other Expenses (e.g. tolls)		D / F (Km/L or MPG)
				Amount	Cost	Amount	Cost	Cost	Item	

The information recorded on this page and the page above are accurate. Signature:							
	Totals this page:						
	Totals brought forward:						Total Cost: (A+B+C)
	Totals to Date:		A		B	C	

Vehicle Use Log — Year:

Trip No.	Date	Driver's Name / Signature	Trip		Odometer		Distance		
			From	To	Departure	Arrival	Business	Private	**Total**

The sums of the Business and Private distances driven must equal the **Total** distances recorded. Use the **Trips Details** page (below) to record more information (as necessary) about the Trips logged on this page. Make sure that the **Trip No.**s are identical on both pages, in order to be clear as to which Trip the Details refer.	% of **Total** distance driven that was for business: ______%	% of **Total** distance driven that was private: ______%	Calculate, using data from the **Trips Details** page: Business costs total: ______ Private costs total: ______	Totals this page: Totals brought forward: **Totals to Date:**	Business	Private	Total

Trips Details

Trip No.	**Purpose of Trip / Incidents Y/N** (incidents could be accidents, malfunctions, etc - enter Y or N here. Explain on the corresponding Technical Incidents Log page, as required)	**Odometer** (at time of fuel or oil added)	**Distance** (since last refuel)	**Oil Added**		**Fuel Added**		**Other Expenses** (e.g. tolls)		**D / F** (Km/L or MPG)
				Amount	Cost	Amount	Cost	Cost	Item	

The information recorded on this page and the page above are accurate. Signature:

	Oil Amount	Oil Cost	Fuel Amount	Fuel Cost	Other Cost	
Totals this page:						
Totals brought forward:						**Total Cost:** (A+B+C)
Totals to Date:		A		B	C	

VEHICLE USE LOG   YEAR:

Trip No.	Date	Driver's Name / Signature	Trip		Odometer		Distance		
			From	To	Departure	Arrival	Business	Private	**Total**

Notes	% of **Total** distance driven that was for business:	% of **Total** distance driven that was private:	Calculate, using data from the **Trips Details** page: Business costs total:	Private costs total:	Totals	Business	Private	Total
The sums of the Business and Private distances driven must equal the **Total** distances recorded. Use the **Trips Details** page (below) to record more information (as necessary) about the Trips logged on this page. Make sure that the **Trip No.**s are identical on both pages, in order to be clear as to which Trip the Details refer.	______%	______%	________	________	Totals this page:			
					Totals brought forward:			
					Totals to Date:			

TRIPS DETAILS

Trip No.	Purpose of Trip / Incidents Y/N (incidents could be accidents, malfunctions, etc - enter Y or N here. Explain on the corresponding Technical Incidents Log page, as required)	Odometer (at time of fuel or oil added)	Distance (since last refuel)	Oil Added		Fuel Added		Other Expenses (e.g. tolls)		D / F (Km/L or MPG)
				Amount	Cost	Amount	Cost	Cost	Item	

The information recorded on this page and the page above are accurate. Signature:								
	Totals this page:							
	Totals brought forward:							Total Cost: (A+B+C)
	Totals to Date:		A		B	C		

VEHICLE USE LOG   YEAR:

Trip No.	Date	Driver's Name / Signature	Trip		Odometer		Distance		
			From	To	Departure	Arrival	Business	Private	**Total**

Notes	% of **Total** distance driven that was for business:	% of **Total** distance driven that was private:	Calculate, using data from the **Trips Details** page: Business costs total:	Private costs total:		Business	Private	Total
The sums of the Business and Private distances driven must equal the **Total** distances recorded. Use the **Trips Details** page (below) to record more information (as necessary) about the Trips logged on this page. Make sure that the **Trip No.**s are identical on both pages, in order to be clear as to which Trip the Details refer.	______%	______%	______	______	Totals this page:			
					Totals brought forward:			
					Totals to Date:			

TRIPS DETAILS

Trip No.	Purpose of Trip / Incidents Y/N (incidents could be accidents, malfunctions, etc - enter Y or N here. Explain on the corresponding Technical Incidents Log page, as required)	Odometer (at time of fuel or oil added)	Distance (since last refuel)	Oil Added		Fuel Added		Other Expenses (e.g. tolls)		D / F (Km/L or MPG)
				Amount	Cost	Amount	Cost	Cost	Item	

The information recorded on this page and the page above are accurate. Signature:							
	Totals this page:						
	Totals brought forward:						**Total Cost:** (A+B+C)
	Totals to Date:		A		B	C	

VEHICLE USE LOG   YEAR:

Trip No.	Date	Driver's Name / Signature	Trip		Odometer		Distance		
			From	To	Departure	Arrival	Business	Private	**Total**

The sums of the Business and Private distances driven must equal the **Total** distances recorded. Use the **Trips Details** page (below) to record more information (as necessary) about the Trips logged on this page. Make sure that the **Trip No.**s are identical on both pages, in order to be clear as to which Trip the Details refer.	% of **Total** distance driven that was for business: ______%	% of **Total** distance driven that was private: ______%	Calculate, using data from the **Trips Details** page: Business costs total: ________	Private costs total: ________	Totals this page:			
					Totals brought forward:			
					Totals to Date:			

Trips Details

Trip No.	Purpose of Trip / Incidents Y/N (incidents could be accidents, malfunctions, etc - enter Y or N here. Explain on the corresponding Technical Incidents Log page, as required)	Odometer (at time of fuel or oil added)	Distance (since last refuel)	Oil Added		Fuel Added		Other Expenses (e.g. tolls)		D / F (Km/L or MPG)
				Amount	Cost	Amount	Cost	Cost	Item	

The information recorded on this page and the page above are accurate. Signature:

____

	Oil Added Amount	Oil Added Cost	Fuel Added Amount	Fuel Added Cost	Other Expenses Cost	
Totals this page:						
Totals brought forward:						**Total Cost:** (A+B+C)
Totals to Date:		A		B	C	

VEHICLE USE LOG　　　YEAR:

Trip No.	Date	Driver's Name / Signature	Trip		Odometer		Distance		
			From	To	Departure	Arrival	Business	Private	**Total**

The sums of the Business and Private distances driven must equal the **Total** distances recorded.

Use the **Trips Details** page (below) to record more information (as necessary) about the Trips logged on this page. Make sure that the **Trip No.**s are identical on both pages, in order to be clear as to which Trip the Details refer.

% of **Total** distance driven that was for business:	% of **Total** distance driven that was private:	Calculate, using data from the **Trips Details** page: Business costs total:	Private costs total:
_______%	_______%	________	________

	Business	Private	Total
Totals this page:			
Totals brought forward:			
Totals to Date:			

Trips Details

Trip No.	Purpose of Trip / Incidents Y/N (incidents could be accidents, malfunctions, etc - enter Y or N here. Explain on the corresponding Technical Incidents Log page, as required)	Odometer (at time of fuel or oil added)	Distance (since last refuel)	Oil Added		Fuel Added		Other Expenses (e.g. tolls)		D / F (Km/L or MPG)
				Amount	Cost	Amount	Cost	Cost	Item	

The information recorded on this page and the page above are accurate. Signature:							
	Totals this page:						
	Totals brought forward:						**Total Cost:** (A+B+C)
	Totals to Date:		A		B	C	

Vehicle Use Log — Year:

Trip No.	Date	Driver's Name / Signature	Trip		Odometer		Distance		
			From	To	Departure	Arrival	Business	Private	**Total**

The sums of the Business and Private distances driven must equal the **Total** distances recorded. Use the **Trips Details** page (below) to record more information (as necessary) about the Trips logged on this page. Make sure that the **Trip No.**s are identical on both pages, in order to be clear as to which Trip the Details refer.	% of **Total** distance driven that was for business: _____%	% of **Total** distance driven that was private: _____%	Calculate, using data from the **Trips Details** page: Business costs total: _____	Private costs total: _____	Totals this page:			
					Totals brought forward:			
					Totals to Date:			

Trips Details

Trip No.	Purpose of Trip / Incidents Y/N (incidents could be accidents, malfunctions, etc - enter Y or N here. Explain on the corresponding Technical Incidents Log page, as required)	Odometer (at time of fuel or oil added)	Distance (since last refuel)	Oil Added		Fuel Added		Other Expenses (e.g. tolls)		D / F (Km/L or MPG)
				Amount	Cost	Amount	Cost	Cost	Item	

The information recorded on this page and the page above are accurate. Signature:							
	Totals this page:						
	Totals brought forward:						Total Cost: (A+B+C)
	Totals to Date:		A		B	C	

Vehicle Use Log Year:

Trip No.	Date	Driver's Name / Signature	Trip		Odometer		Distance		
			From	To	Departure	Arrival	Business	Private	**Total**

The sums of the Business and Private distances driven must equal the **Total** distances recorded. Use the **Trips Details** page (below) to record more information (as necessary) about the Trips logged on this page. Make sure that the **Trip No.**s are identical on both pages, in order to be clear as to which Trip the Details refer.	% of **Total** distance driven that was for business: ______%	% of **Total** distance driven that was private: ______%	Calculate, using data from the **Trips Details** page: Business costs total: ______	Private costs total: ______	Totals this page:			
					Totals brought forward:			
					Totals to Date:			

TRIPS DETAILS

Trip No.	Purpose of Trip / Incidents Y/N (incidents could be accidents, malfunctions, etc - enter Y or N here. Explain on the corresponding Technical Incidents Log page, as required)	Odometer (at time of fuel or oil added)	Distance (since last refuel)	Oil Added		Fuel Added		Other Expenses (e.g. tolls)		D / F (Km/L or MPG)
				Amount	Cost	Amount	Cost	Cost	Item	

The information recorded on this page and the page above are accurate. Signature:								
	Totals this page:							
	Totals brought forward:						Total Cost: (A+B+C)	
	Totals to Date:		A		B	C		

Vehicle Use Log

Year:

Trip No.	Date	Driver's Name / Signature	Trip		Odometer		Distance		
			From	To	Departure	Arrival	Business	Private	**Total**

The sums of the Business and Private distances driven must equal the **Total** distances recorded.

Use the **Trips Details** page (below) to record more information (as necessary) about the Trips logged on this page. Make sure that the **Trip No.**s are identical on both pages, in order to be clear as to which Trip the Details refer.

% of **Total** distance driven that was for business:	% of **Total** distance driven that was private:	Calculate, using data from the **Trips Details** page: Business costs total:	Private costs total:		Business	Private	Total
______%	______%	______	______	Totals this page:			
				Totals brought forward:			
				Totals to Date:			

TRIPS DETAILS

Trip No.	Purpose of Trip / Incidents Y/N (incidents could be accidents, malfunctions, etc - enter Y or N here. Explain on the corresponding Technical Incidents Log page, as required)	Odometer (at time of fuel or oil added)	Distance (since last refuel)	Oil Added		Fuel Added		Other Expenses (e.g. tolls)		D / F (Km/L or MPG)
				Amount	Cost	Amount	Cost	Cost	Item	

The information recorded on this page and the page above are accurate. Signature:		Oil Amount	Oil Cost	Fuel Amount	Fuel Cost	Other Cost	
	Totals this page:						
	Totals brought forward:						**Total Cost:** (A+B+C)
	Totals to Date:		A		B	C	

Vehicle Use Log

Year:

Trip No.	Date	Driver's Name / Signature	Trip		Odometer		Distance		
			From	To	Departure	Arrival	Business	Private	**Total**

The sums of the Business and Private distances driven must equal the **Total** distances recorded. Use the **Trips Details** page (below) to record more information (as necessary) about the Trips logged on this page. Make sure that the **Trip No.**s are identical on both pages, in order to be clear as to which Trip the Details refer.	% of **Total** distance driven that was for business: ______%	% of **Total** distance driven that was private: ______%	Calculate, using data from the **Trips Details** page: Business costs total: ______	Private costs total: ______	Totals this page:			
					Totals brought forward:			
					Totals to Date:			

Trips Details

Trip No.	Purpose of Trip / Incidents Y/N (Incidents could be accidents, malfunctions, etc - enter Y or N here. Explain on the corresponding Technical Incidents Log page, as required)	Odometer (at time of fuel or oil added)	Distance (since last refuel)	Oil Added		Fuel Added		Other Expenses (e.g. tolls)		D / F (Km/L or MPG)
				Amount	Cost	Amount	Cost	Cost	Item	

The information recorded on this page and the page above are accurate. Signature:		Oil Amount	Oil Cost	Fuel Amount	Fuel Cost	Other Cost	
	Totals this page:						
	Totals brought forward:						**Total Cost:** (A+B+C)
	Totals to Date:		A		B	C	

VEHICLE USE LOG   YEAR:

Trip No.	Date	Driver's Name / Signature	Trip		Odometer		Distance		
			From	To	Departure	Arrival	Business	Private	**Total**

The sums of the Business and Private distances driven must equal the **Total** distances recorded. Use the **Trips Details** page (below) to record more information (as necessary) about the Trips logged on this page. Make sure that the **Trip No.**s are identical on both pages, in order to be clear as to which Trip the Details refer.	% of **Total** distance driven that was for business: ______%	% of **Total** distance driven that was private: ______%	Calculate, using data from the **Trips Details** page: Business costs total: ________	Private costs total: ________	Totals this page:			
					Totals brought forward:			
					Totals to Date:			

Trips Details

Trip No.	Purpose of Trip / Incidents Y/N (incidents could be accidents, malfunctions, etc - enter Y or N here. Explain on the corresponding Technical Incidents Log page, as required)	Odometer (at time of fuel or oil added)	Distance (since last refuel)	Oil Added		Fuel Added		Other Expenses (e.g. tolls)		D / F (Km/L or MPG)
				Amount	Cost	Amount	Cost	Cost	Item	

The information recorded on this page and the page above are accurate. Signature:							
	Totals this page:						
	Totals brought forward:						Total Cost: (A+B+C)
	Totals to Date:		A		B	C	

VEHICLE USE LOG YEAR:

Trip No.	Date	Driver's Name / Signature	Trip		Odometer		Distance		
			From	To	Departure	Arrival	Business	Private	**Total**

The sums of the Business and Private distances driven must equal the **Total** distances recorded.

Use the **Trips Details** page (below) to record more information (as necessary) about the Trips logged on this page. Make sure that the **Trip No.**s are identical on both pages, in order to be clear as to which Trip the Details refer.

% of **Total** distance driven that was for business: ______%

% of **Total** distance driven that was private: ______%

Calculate, using data from the **Trips Details** page:

Business costs total: ________

Private costs total: ________

	Business	Private	Total
Totals this page:			
Totals brought forward:			
Totals to Date:			

Trips Details

Trip No.	Purpose of Trip / Incidents Y/N (incidents could be accidents, malfunctions, etc enter Y or N here. Explain on the corresponding Technical Incidents Log page, as required)	Odometer (at time of fuel or oil added)	Distance (since last refuel)	Oil Added		Fuel Added		Other Expenses (e.g. tolls)		D / F (Km/L or MPG)
				Amount	Cost	Amount	Cost	Cost	Item	
The information recorded on this page and the page above are accurate. Signature:			Totals this page:							
			Totals brought forward:						**Total Cost:** (A+B+C)	
			Totals to Date:		A		B	C		

VEHICLE USE LOG   YEAR:

Trip No.	Date	Driver's Name / Signature	Trip		Odometer		Distance		
			From	To	Departure	Arrival	Business	Private	**Total**

The sums of the Business and Private distances driven must equal the **Total** distances recorded. Use the **Trips Details** page (below) to record more information (as necessary) about the Trips logged on this page. Make sure that the **Trip No.**s are identical on both pages, in order to be clear as to which Trip the Details refer.	% of **Total** distance driven that was for business: ______%	% of **Total** distance driven that was private: ______%	Calculate, using data from the **Trips Details** page: Business costs total: ______	Private costs total: ______	Totals this page:			
					Totals brought forward:			
					Totals to Date:			

TRIPS DETAILS

Trip No.	Purpose of Trip / Incidents Y/N (Incidents could be accidents, malfunctions, etc - enter Y or N here. Explain on the corresponding Technical Incidents Log page, as required)	Odometer (at time of fuel or oil added)	Distance (since last refuel)	Oil Added		Fuel Added		Other Expenses (e.g. tolls)		D / F (Km/L or MPG)
				Amount	Cost	Amount	Cost	Cost	Item	
The information recorded on this page and the page above are accurate. Signature:		Totals this page:								
		Totals brought forward:							**Total Cost:** (A+B+C)	
		Totals to Date:			A		B	C		

VEHICLE USE LOG YEAR:

Trip No.	Date	Driver's Name / Signature	Trip		Odometer		Distance		
			From	To	Departure	Arrival	Business	Private	**Total**

The sums of the Business and Private distances driven must equal the **Total** distances recorded.

Use the **Trips Details** page (below) to record more information (as necessary) about the Trips logged on this page. Make sure that the **Trip No.**s are identical on both pages, in order to be clear as to which Trip the Details refer.

% of **Total** distance driven that was for business:	% of **Total** distance driven that was private:	Calculate, using data from the **Trips Details** page: Business costs total:	Private costs total:
_____%	_____%	_______	_______

	Business	Private	Total
Totals this page:			
Totals brought forward:			
Totals to Date:			

TRIPS DETAILS

Trip No.	Purpose of Trip / Incidents Y/N (incidents could be accidents, malfunctions, etc - enter Y or N here. Explain on the corresponding Technical Incidents Log page, as required)	Odometer (at time of fuel or oil added)	Distance (since last refuel)	Oil Added		Fuel Added		Other Expenses (e.g. tolls)		D / F (Km/L or MPG)
				Amount	Cost	Amount	Cost	Cost	Item	

The information recorded on this page and the page above are accurate. Signature:		Oil Amount	Oil Cost	Fuel Amount	Fuel Cost	Other Cost	
	Totals this page:						
	Totals brought forward:						Total Cost: (A+B+C)
	Totals to Date:		A		B	C	

VEHICLE USE LOG   YEAR:

Trip No.	Date	Driver's Name / Signature	Trip		Odometer		Distance		
			From	To	Departure	Arrival	Business	Private	**Total**

The sums of the Business and Private distances driven must equal the **Total** distances recorded. Use the **Trips Details** page (below) to record more information (as necessary) about the Trips logged on this page. Make sure that the **Trip No.**s are identical on both pages, in order to be clear as to which Trip the Details refer.	% of **Total** distance driven that was for business: ______%	% of **Total** distance driven that was private: ______%	Calculate, using data from the **Trips Details** page: Business costs total: ________	Private costs total: ________	Totals this page:			
					Totals brought forward:			
					Totals to Date:			

Trips Details

Trip No.	Purpose of Trip / Incidents Y/N (incidents could be accidents, malfunctions, etc - enter Y or N here. Explain on the corresponding Technical Incidents Log page, as required)	Odometer (at time of fuel or oil added)	Distance (since last refuel)	Oil Added		Fuel Added		Other Expenses (e.g. tolls)		D / F (Km/L or MPG)
				Amount	Cost	Amount	Cost	Cost	Item	
The information recorded on this page and the page above are accurate. Signature:			Totals this page:							
			Totals brought forward:						Total Cost: (A+B+C)	
			Totals to Date:		A		B	C		

VEHICLE USE LOG YEAR:

Trip No.	Date	Driver's Name / Signature	Trip		Odometer		Distance		
			From	To	Departure	Arrival	Business	Private	**Total**

The sums of the Business and Private distances driven must equal the **Total** distances recorded.

Use the **Trips Details** page (below) to record more information (as necessary) about the Trips logged on this page. Make sure that the **Trip No.**s are identical on both pages, in order to be clear as to which Trip the Details refer.

% of **Total** distance driven that was for business: ______%

% of **Total** distance driven that was private: ______%

Calculate, using data from the **Trips Details** page:

Business costs total: ______

Private costs total: ______

	Business	Private	Total
Totals this page:			
Totals brought forward:			
Totals to Date:			

Trips Details

Trip No.	Purpose of Trip / Incidents Y/N (incidents could be accidents, malfunctions, etc - enter Y or N here. Explain on the corresponding Technical Incidents Log page, as required)	Odometer (at time of fuel or oil added)	Distance (since last refuel)	Oil Added		Fuel Added		Other Expenses (e.g. tolls)		D / F (Km/L or MPG)
				Amount	Cost	Amount	Cost	Cost	Item	

The information recorded on this page and the page above are accurate. Signature:		Oil Amount	Oil Cost	Fuel Amount	Fuel Cost	Other Cost	
	Totals this page:						
	Totals brought forward:						**Total Cost:** (A+B+C)
	Totals to Date:		A		B	C	

VEHICLE USE LOG   YEAR:

Trip No.	Date	Driver's Name / Signature	Trip		Odometer		Distance		
			From	To	Departure	Arrival	Business	Private	**Total**

The sums of the Business and Private distances driven must equal the **Total** distances recorded. Use the **Trips Details** page (below) to record more information (as necessary) about the Trips logged on this page. Make sure that the **Trip No.**s are identical on both pages, in order to be clear as to which Trip the Details refer.	% of **Total** distance driven that was for business: ______%	% of **Total** distance driven that was private: ______%	Calculate, using data from the **Trips Details** page: Business costs total: ________	Private costs total: ________	Totals this page:			
					Totals brought forward:			
					Totals to Date:			

TRIPS DETAILS

Trip No.	Purpose of Trip / Incidents Y/N (incidents could be accidents, malfunctions, etc - enter Y or N here. Explain on the corresponding Technical Incidents Log page, as required)	Odometer (at time of fuel or oil added)	Distance (since last refuel)	Oil Added		Fuel Added		Other Expenses (e.g. tolls)		D / F (Km/L or MPG)
				Amount	Cost	Amount	Cost	Cost	Item	

The information recorded on this page and the page above are accurate. Signature:							
	Totals this page:						
	Totals brought forward:						Total Cost: (A+B+C)
	Totals to Date:		A		B	C	

VEHICLE USE LOG YEAR:

Trip No.	Date	Driver's Name / Signature	Trip		Odometer		Distance		
			From	To	Departure	Arrival	Business	Private	**Total**

The sums of the Business and Private distances driven must equal the **Total** distances recorded.

Use the **Trips Details** page (below) to record more information (as necessary) about the Trips logged on this page. Make sure that the **Trip No.**s are identical on both pages, in order to be clear as to which Trip the Details refer.

% of **Total** distance driven that was for business: ______%

% of **Total** distance driven that was private: ______%

Calculate, using data from the **Trips Details** page:

Business costs total: ______

Private costs total: ______

	Business	Private	Total
Totals this page:			
Totals brought forward:			
Totals to Date:			

Trips Details

Trip No.	Purpose of Trip / Incidents Y/N (incidents could be accidents, malfunctions, etc - enter Y or N here. Explain on the corresponding Technical Incidents Log page, as required)	Odometer (at time of fuel or oil added)	Distance (since last refuel)	Oil Added		Fuel Added		Other Expenses (e.g. tolls)		D / F (Km/L or MPG)
				Amount	Cost	Amount	Cost	Cost	Item	
The information recorded on this page and the page above are accurate. Signature:		Totals this page:								
		Totals brought forward:							Total Cost: (A+B+C)	
		Totals to Date:			A		B	C		

VEHICLE USE LOG   YEAR:

Trip No.	Date	Driver's Name / Signature	Trip		Odometer		Distance		
			From	To	Departure	Arrival	Business	Private	**Total**

The sums of the Business and Private distances driven must equal the **Total** distances recorded. Use the **Trips Details** page (below) to record more information (as necessary) about the Trips logged on this page. Make sure that the **Trip No.**s are identical on both pages, in order to be clear as to which Trip the Details refer.	% of **Total** distance driven that was for business: _____%	% of **Total** distance driven that was private: _____%	Calculate, using data from the **Trips Details** page: Business costs total: _____	Private costs total: _____	Totals this page: Totals brought forward: **Totals to Date:**			

TRIPS DETAILS

Trip No.	**Purpose of Trip / Incidents Y/N** (incidents could be accidents, malfunctions, etc - enter Y or N here. Explain on the corresponding Technical Incidents Log page, as required)	**Odometer** (at time of fuel or oil added)	**Distance** (since last refuel)	**Oil Added**		**Fuel Added**		**Other Expenses** (e.g. tolls)		**D / F** (Km/L or MPG)
				Amount	Cost	Amount	Cost	Cost	Item	
The information recorded on this page and the page above are accurate. Signature:		Totals this page:								
		Totals brought forward:							**Total Cost:** (A+B+C)	
		Totals to Date:			A		B	C		

VEHICLE USE LOG YEAR:

Trip No.	Date	Driver's Name / Signature	Trip		Odometer		Distance		
			From	To	Departure	Arrival	Business	Private	**Total**

The sums of the Business and Private distances driven must equal the **Total** distances recorded. Use the **Trips Details** page (below) to record more information (as necessary) about the Trips logged on this page. Make sure that the **Trip No.**s are identical on both pages, in order to be clear as to which Trip the Details refer.	% of **Total** distance driven that was for business: _______%	% of **Total** distance driven that was private: _______%	Calculate, using data from the **Trips Details** page: Business costs total: _________	Private costs total: _________	Totals this page:		
					Totals brought forward:		
					Totals to Date:		

Trips Details

Trip No.	**Purpose of Trip / Incidents Y/N** (incidents could be accidents, malfunctions, etc - enter Y or N here. Explain on the corresponding Technical Incidents Log page, as required)	**Odometer** (at time of fuel or oil added)	**Distance** (since last refuel)	**Oil Added**		**Fuel Added**		**Other Expenses** (e.g. tolls)		**D / F** (Km/L or MPG)
				Amount	Cost	Amount	Cost	Cost	Item	

The information recorded on this page and the page above are accurate. Signature:		Oil Amount	Oil Cost	Fuel Amount	Fuel Cost	Other Cost	
	Totals this page:						
	Totals brought forward:						**Total Cost:** (A+B+C)
	Totals to Date:		A		B	C	

VEHICLE USE LOG YEAR:

Trip No.	Date	Driver's Name / Signature	Trip		Odometer		Distance		
			From	To	Departure	Arrival	Business	Private	**Total**

The sums of the Business and Private distances driven must equal the **Total** distances recorded.

Use the **Trips Details** page (below) to record more information (as necessary) about the Trips logged on this page. Make sure that the **Trip No.**s are identical on both pages, in order to be clear as to which Trip the Details refer.

% of **Total** distance driven that was for business:	% of **Total** distance driven that was private:	Calculate, using data from the **Trips Details** page: Business costs total:	Private costs total:
______%	______%	______	______

	Business	Private	Total
Totals this page:			
Totals brought forward:			
Totals to Date:			

Trips Details

Trip No.	Purpose of Trip / Incidents Y/N (incidents could be accidents, malfunctions, etc - enter Y or N here. Explain on the corresponding Technical Incidents Log page, as required)	Odometer (at time of fuel or oil added)	Distance (since last refuel)	Oil Added		Fuel Added		Other Expenses (e.g. tolls)		D / F (Km/L or MPG)
				Amount	Cost	Amount	Cost	Cost	Item	
The information recorded on this page and the page above are accurate. Signature:		Totals this page:								
		Totals brought forward:							Total Cost: (A+B+C)	
		Totals to Date:			A		B	C		

VEHICLE USE LOG YEAR:

Trip No.	Date	Driver's Name / Signature	Trip		Odometer		Distance		
			From	To	Departure	Arrival	Business	Private	**Total**

The sums of the Business and Private distances driven must equal the **Total** distances recorded. Use the **Trips Details** page (below) to record more information (as necessary) about the Trips logged on this page. Make sure that the **Trip No.**s are identical on both pages, in order to be clear as to which Trip the Details refer.	% of **Total** distance driven that was for business: ______%	% of **Total** distance driven that was private: ______%	Calculate, using data from the **Trips Details** page: Business costs total: ________	Private costs total: ________	Totals this page:			
					Totals brought forward:			
					Totals to Date:			

Trips Details

Trip No.	Purpose of Trip / Incidents Y/N (incidents could be accidents, malfunctions, etc - enter Y or N here. Explain on the corresponding Technical Incidents Log page, as required)	Odometer (at time of fuel or oil added)	Distance (since last refuel)	Oil Added		Fuel Added		Other Expenses (e.g. tolls)		D / F (Km/L or MPG)
				Amount	Cost	Amount	Cost	Cost	Item	

The information recorded on this page and the page above are accurate. Signature:

____

	Oil Amount	Oil Cost	Fuel Amount	Fuel Cost	Other Cost	
Totals this page:						
Totals brought forward:						**Total Cost:** (A+B+C)
Totals to Date:		A		B	C	

Vehicle Use Log — Year:

Trip No.	Date	Driver's Name / Signature	Trip		Odometer		Distance		
			From	To	Departure	Arrival	Business	Private	**Total**

The sums of the Business and Private distances driven must equal the **Total** distances recorded. Use the **Trips Details** page (below) to record more information (as necessary) about the Trips logged on this page. Make sure that the **Trip No.**s are identical on both pages, in order to be clear as to which Trip the Details refer.	% of **Total** distance driven that was for business: _______%	% of **Total** distance driven that was private: _______%	Calculate, using data from the **Trips Details** page: Business costs total: __________	Private costs total: __________			
					Totals this page:		
					Totals brought forward:		
					Totals to Date:		

Trips Details

Trip No.	Purpose of Trip / Incidents Y/N (incidents could be accidents, malfunctions, etc - enter Y or N here. Explain on the corresponding Technical Incidents Log page, as required)	Odometer (at time of fuel or oil added)	Distance (since last refuel)	Oil Added		Fuel Added		Other Expenses (e.g. tolls)		D / F (Km/L or MPG)
				Amount	Cost	Amount	Cost	Cost	Item	

The information recorded on this page and the page above are accurate. Signature:							
	Totals this page:						
	Totals brought forward:						Total Cost: (A+B+C)
	Totals to Date:		A		B	C	

Vehicle Use Log   Year:

Trip No.	Date	Driver's Name / Signature	Trip		Odometer		Distance		
			From	To	Departure	Arrival	Business	Private	**Total**

The sums of the Business and Private distances driven must equal the **Total** distances recorded. Use the **Trips Details** page (below) to record more information (as necessary) about the Trips logged on this page. Make sure that the **Trip No.**s are identical on both pages, in order to be clear as to which Trip the Details refer.	% of **Total** distance driven that was for business: ______%	% of **Total** distance driven that was private: ______%	Calculate, using data from the **Trips Details** page: Business costs total: ______	Private costs total: ______	Totals this page:			
					Totals brought forward:			
					Totals to Date:			

Trips Details

Trip No.	Purpose of Trip / Incidents Y/N (incidents could be accidents, malfunctions, etc - enter Y or N here. Explain on the corresponding Technical Incidents Log page, as required)	Odometer (at time of fuel or oil added)	Distance (since last refuel)	Oil Added		Fuel Added		Other Expenses (e.g. tolls)		D / F (Km/L or MPG)
				Amount	Cost	Amount	Cost	Cost	Item	

The information recorded on this page and the page above are accurate. Signature:

	Oil Amount	Oil Cost	Fuel Amount	Fuel Cost	Other Cost	
Totals this page:						
Totals brought forward:						**Total Cost:** (A+B+C)
Totals to Date:		A		B	C	

VEHICLE USE LOG YEAR:

Trip No.	Date	Driver's Name / Signature	Trip		Odometer		Distance		
			From	To	Departure	Arrival	Business	Private	**Total**

The sums of the Business and Private distances driven must equal the **Total** distances recorded. Use the **Trips Details** page (below) to record more information (as necessary) about the Trips logged on this page. Make sure that the **Trip No.**s are identical on both pages, in order to be clear as to which Trip the Details refer.	% of **Total** distance driven that was for business: _______%	% of **Total** distance driven that was private: _______%	Calculate, using data from the **Trips Details** page: Business costs total: ________	Private costs total: ________			
					Totals this page:			
					Totals brought forward:			
					Totals to Date:			

Trips Details

Trip No.	**Purpose of Trip / Incidents Y/N** (incidents could be accidents, malfunctions, etc - enter Y or N here. Explain on the corresponding Technical Incidents Log page, as required)	**Odometer** (at time of fuel or oil added)	**Distance** (since last refuel)	**Oil Added**		**Fuel Added**		**Other Expenses** (e.g. tolls)		**D / F** (Km/L or MPG)
				Amount	Cost	Amount	Cost	Cost	Item	

The information recorded on this page and the page above are accurate. Signature:	Totals this page:							
	Totals brought forward:						**Total Cost:** (A+B+C)	
______________________	**Totals to Date:**		A		B	C		

VEHICLE USE LOG YEAR:

Trip No.	Date	Driver's Name / Signature	Trip		Odometer		Distance		
			From	To	Departure	Arrival	Business	Private	**Total**

						Business	Private	Total
The sums of the Business and Private distances driven must equal the **Total** distances recorded. Use the **Trips Details** page (below) to record more information (as necessary) about the Trips logged on this page. Make sure that the **Trip No.**s are identical on both pages, in order to be clear as to which Trip the Details refer.	% of **Total** distance driven that was for business: _______%	% of **Total** distance driven that was private: _______%	Calculate, using data from the **Trips Details** page: Business costs total: ________	Private costs total: ________	Totals this page:			
					Totals brought forward:			
					Totals to Date:			

Trips Details

Trip No.	Purpose of Trip / Incidents Y/N (incidents could be accidents, malfunctions, etc - enter Y or N here. Explain on the corresponding Technical Incidents Log page, as required)	Odometer (at time of fuel or oil added)	Distance (since last refuel)	Oil Added		Fuel Added		Other Expenses (e.g. tolls)		D / F (Km/L or MPG)
				Amount	Cost	Amount	Cost	Cost	Item	

The information recorded on this page and the page above are accurate. Signature:		Oil Amount	Oil Cost	Fuel Amount	Fuel Cost	Other Cost	
	Totals this page:						
	Totals brought forward:						Total Cost: (A+B+C)
	Totals to Date:		A		B	C	

VEHICLE USE LOG YEAR:

Trip No.	Date	Driver's Name / Signature	Trip		Odometer		Distance		
			From	To	Departure	Arrival	Business	Private	**Total**

The sums of the Business and Private distances driven must equal the **Total** distances recorded. Use the **Trips Details** page (below) to record more information (as necessary) about the Trips logged on this page. Make sure that the **Trip No.**s are identical on both pages, in order to be clear as to which Trip the Details refer.	% of **Total** distance driven that was for business: ______%	% of **Total** distance driven that was private: ______%	Calculate, using data from the **Trips Details** page: Business costs total: ______	Private costs total: ______	Totals this page:			
					Totals brought forward:			
					Totals to Date:			

Trips Details

Trip No.	**Purpose of Trip / Incidents Y/N** (incidents could be accidents, malfunctions, etc - enter Y or N here, Explain on the corresponding Technical Incidents Log page, as required)	**Odometer** (at time of fuel or oil added)	**Distance** (since last refuel)	**Oil Added**		**Fuel Added**		**Other Expenses** (e.g. tolls)		**D / F** (Km/L or MPG)
				Amount	Cost	Amount	Cost	Cost	Item	

The information recorded on this page and the page above are accurate. Signature:

____

	Oil Amount	Oil Cost	Fuel Amount	Fuel Cost	Other Cost	
Totals this page:						
Totals brought forward:						**Total Cost:** (A+B+C)
Totals to Date:		A		B	C	

VEHICLE USE LOG YEAR:

Trip No.	Date	Driver's Name / Signature	Trip		Odometer		Distance		
			From	To	Departure	Arrival	Business	Private	**Total**

The sums of the Business and Private distances driven must equal the **Total** distances recorded.

Use the **Trips Details** page (below) to record more information (as necessary) about the Trips logged on this page. Make sure that the **Trip No.**s are identical on both pages, in order to be clear as to which Trip the Details refer.

% of **Total** distance driven that was for business: ______%

% of **Total** distance driven that was private: ______%

Calculate, using data from the **Trips Details** page:

Business costs total: ______

Private costs total: ______

	Business	Private	Total
Totals this page:			
Totals brought forward:			
Totals to Date:			

Trips Details

Trip No.	Purpose of Trip / Incidents Y/N (incidents could be accidents, malfunctions, etc enter Y or N here. Explain on the corresponding Technical Incidents Log page, as required)	Odometer (at time of fuel or oil added)	Distance (since last refuel)	Oil Added		Fuel Added		Other Expenses (e.g. tolls)		D / F (Km/L or MPG)
				Amount	Cost	Amount	Cost	Cost	Item	

The information recorded on this page and the page above are accurate. Signature:

	Oil Amount	Oil Cost	Fuel Amount	Fuel Cost	Other Cost	
Totals this page:						
Totals brought forward:						**Total Cost:** (A+B+C)
Totals to Date:		A		B	C	

Trips Notes

Part 3: Maintenance and Inspections

Technical Incidents Log

Event No.	**Trip No.**	**Date**	**Odometer** (at time of incident)	**Driver**	**Incident Description** (accident, malfunction, etc)

Technical Incidents Log

Event No.	Trip No.	Date	Odometer (at time of incident)	Driver	Incident Description (accident, malfunction, etc)

Technical Incidents Log

Event No.	Trip No.	Date	**Odometer** (at time of incident)	Driver	**Incident Description** (accident, malfunction, etc)

Technical Incidents Log

Event No.	Trip No.	Date	Odometer (at time of incident)	Driver	Incident Description (accident, malfunction, etc)

Maintenance Log

Date	Maintenance Actions / Vehicle Improvements / Equipment Change	Vendor / Mechanic	Cost

Maintenance Log

Date	Maintenance Actions / Vehicle Improvements / Equipment Change	Vendor / Mechanic	Cost

Maintenance Log

Date	Maintenance Actions / Vehicle Improvements / Equipment Change	Vendor / Mechanic	Cost

Maintenance Log

Date	Maintenance Actions / Vehicle Improvements / Equipment Change	Vendor / Mechanic	Cost

Maintenance Log

Date	Maintenance Actions / Vehicle Improvements / Equipment Change	Vendor / Mechanic	Cost

Maintenance Log

Date	Maintenance Actions / Vehicle Improvements / Equipment Change	Vendor / Mechanic	Cost

INSPECTIONS LOG

Date	Type of Inspection	Authority / Location	**Result** (e.g. Pass / Fail, details)

Inspections Log

Date	Type of Inspection	Authority / Location	**Result** (e.g. Pass / Fail, details)

Inspections Log

Date	Type of Inspection	Authority / Location	**Result** (e.g. Pass / Fail, details)

Part 4: Costs and Efficiency Summary

How to log information in the Costs and Efficiency Summary Log

This section provides a means of summarizing costs and fuel efficiency for given periods of time.

Dates: From / To Enter the date of the period of interest (e.g. the beginning and end of each two pages of the logbook, or the first through the last day of a given month, the first quarter of the year, etc).

Maintenance Costs Calculate the total maintenance costs for the stated period of interest, using data from **Part 3** of this book, and enter that amount here.

Other Costs Calculate the total **Other Expenses** Costs for the stated period of interest, using data from the **Trips Log** pages, and enter that amount here.

Oil Added Calculate the total Amount and Cost of engine oil that was added during the stated period of interest, using data from the **Trips Log** pages, and enter those figures here.

Fuel Added Calculate the total Amount and Cost of fuel that was added during the stated period of interest, using data from the **Trips Log** pages, and enter those figures here.

Distance Driven Calculate the total distance that was driven during the stated period of interest, using data from the **Trips Log** pages, and enter that amount here.

Distance / Fuel Unit Calculate the fuel use per distance for the stated period of interest, using data from the **Trips Log** pages, and enter that figure here.

Costs and Efficiency Summary Log notes continue on the next page →

This section provides a means of summarizing costs and fuel efficiency for given periods of time.

Totals this page: Sum the columns of data entered into a given page and enter those figures in the spaces provided.

Totals brought forward: Copy the **Totals to Date** figures from the PREVIOUS **Costs and Efficiency Summary Log** page and enter them into the spaces provided.

Totals to Date: Sum the 'Totals this page' and 'Totals brought forward' figures and enter the results in the spaces provided. These are your total values over the various periods of interest used. In this way you can see the cost and use of your vehicle over each of the individual periods of interest (e.g. per month or quarter) and can view, as page totals, the cost and use of the vehicle over a set of up to ten such periods.

Total Cost: Sum the **Totals to Date** values labelled A, B, C, D and enter this figure in the box labeled **'Total Cost:'** This represents your total cost for running that vehicle over the entire period of time represented by the ten entries on the page.

This **Summary Log** also permits you to see the total amounts of engine oil and fuel that the vehicle is using over the individual periods of interest, and, in total, over ten such periods per page.

It also allows you to see the rate of fuel use per distance for each of the individual time periods, allowing you to plot the values on a graph and see whether fuel use efficiency is being maintained or not.

Costs and Efficiency Summary Log

Dates: From / To	Maintenance Costs	Other Costs	Oil Added		Fuel Added		Distance Driven (to stated Date)	Distance / Fuel Unit (MPG, Km/L)
			Amount	Cost	Amount	Cost		
Totals this page:								
Totals brought forward:								Total Cost: (A+B+C+D)
Totals to Date:	A	B		C		D		

Costs and Efficiency Summary Log

Dates: From / To	Maintenance Costs	Other Costs	Oil Added		Fuel Added		Distance Driven (to slated Date)	Distance / Fuel Unit (MPG, Km/L)
			Amount	Cost	Amount	Cost		
Totals this page:								
Totals brought forward.								**Total Cost:** (A+B+C+D)
Totals to Date:	A	B		C		D		

Costs and Efficiency Summary Log

Dates: From / To	Maintenance Costs	Other Costs	Oil Added		Fuel Added		Distance Driven (to stated Date)	Distance / Fuel Unit (MPG, Km/L)
			Amount	Cost	Amount	Cost		
Totals this page:								
Totals brought forward:								Total Cost: (A+B+C+D)
Totals to Date:	A	B		C		D		

Costs and Efficiency Summary Log

Dates: From / To	Maintenance Costs	Other Costs	Oil Added		Fuel Added		Distance Driven (to stated **Date**)	Distance / Fuel Unit (MPG, Km/L)
			Amount	Cost	Amount	Cost		
Totals this page:								
Totals brought forward:								**Total Cost:** (A+B+C+D)
Totals to Date:	A	B		C		D		

Costs and Efficiency Summary Log

Dates: From / To	Maintenance Costs	Other Costs	Oil Added		Fuel Added		Distance Driven (to stated Date)	Distance / Fuel Unit (MPG, Km/L)
			Amount	Cost	Amount	Cost		
Totals this page:								
Totals brought forward:								Total Cost: (A+B+C+D)
Totals to Date:	A	B		C		D		

Costs and Efficiency Summary Log

Dates: From / To	Maintenance Costs	Other Costs	Oil Added		Fuel Added		Distance Driven (to stated **Date**)	Distance / Fuel Unit (MPG, Km/L)
			Amount	Cost	Amount	Cost		
Totals this page:								
Totals brought forward:								**Total Cost:** (A+B+C+D)
Totals to Date:	A	B		C		D		

www.ingramcontent.com/pod-product-compliance
Ingram Content Group UK Ltd.
Pitfield, Milton Keynes, MK11 3LW, UK
UKHW021128260726
13994UKWH00001B/34

9 782839 933568